I, Emma

Mirka Anderson

This is a work of nonfiction.

Ordering Information:

Prime Seven Media
518 Landmann St.
Tomah City, WI 54660

Printed in the United States of America

For all persons with Down syndrome,
their families and friends all over the world –
stay positive

Emma

TABLE OF CONTENTS

**Hello ! ! Hola ! Hi ! Cześć ! Ciao ! Hallo ! Bonjour !
Koni'chiwa ! Ni Hao !**

My name is Emma. I live in a town in England called
Royston, near Cambridge with my mum. I am 40 years old
and have two grownup sisters: Caroline and Sophie.

I was born in 1984 in Rosie Hospital in Cambridge.

Now I am an artist and work at the Rowan Foundation studio
in Cambridge creating pieces of art in clay. My greatest
success as an artist was the exhibition of my oil paintings
at the Tate Modern Gallery in London some years ago.

I love dancing, horse riding, working as a volunteer with nursery
children, listening to the 80s music and visiting foreign countries.

My life story is shown in the documentary "the sky
is the limit" made by my mum. We sent it to many
international film festivals. Till now we have had
more than 50 awards from Hawaii to Bhutan.

Royston – the town I live in …

My travels

Chapter 1

FROM BIRTH...

I was born in Cambridge in England. A day after my birth the doctors diagnosed me with the condition known as Down's syndrome and told my parents that they "don't have to take her home as she will not do anything". That was the first negative comment I received from the professionals.

For many months I was struggling with feeding and developing. After one of the visits to my family doctor she discovered that I had a large hole in my heart. I was rushed to the Great Ormond Children's Hospital in London. The operation was done by three surgeons and lasted 8 hours. It was a great success. I started eating and growing fast ...

We lived in a village called Bassingbourn famous for its factory of first London taxis. I liked walks, bike rides and open spaces.

When I was 3 years old I went to the nursery with a helper Gill who supported me through my school years till I was 16. Every school holiday we travelled to Poland to get to know my Polish side of the family and to enjoy their food. I enjoyed playing and learning with my peers.

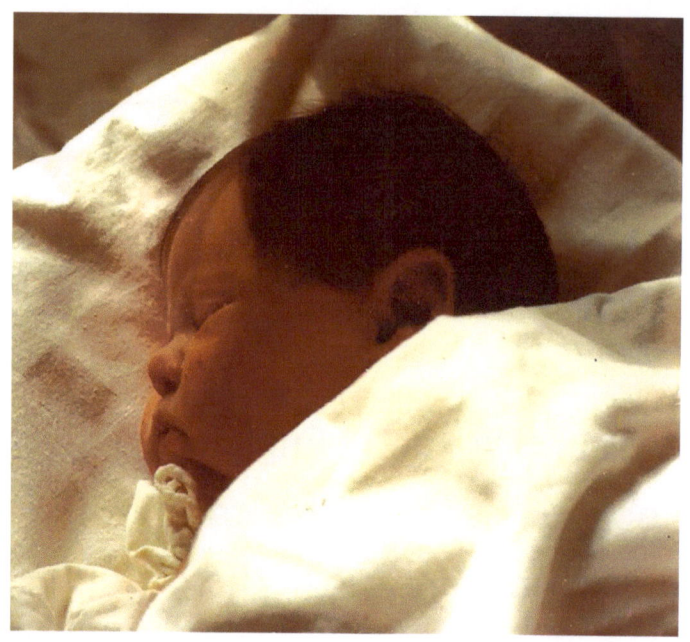

My first day on this planet ...

First snow ...

Don't try to make me smile !

The crumbs and I ...

Chapter 2

MY FAMILY

My father is English and my mother is Polish. She came to England a long time ago. My older sister Caroline was born before me in London. She is an English teacher. My younger sister Sophie was born in Cambridge years after me. She is a nurse. When we were younger, we used to travel a lot together but now we are all grown up and have separate lives.

My mother has been my biggest supporter since birth. She fought for me everywhere so I am included in the community. She helped me with all my problems with health, education, inclusion and social acceptance here, in England, and all over the world.

The village emblem

Our local pub

Chapter 3

SCHOOL YEARS...

I moved to the primary school to learn to read and write. I enjoyed my time there meeting new people, going on outings and getting to know the world around me. I also enjoyed all types of sports. I used to get so excited about the sports days that once I took off in a run race with the boys ! Everyone was laughing but the girls were not happy ...

After school I tried to learn the piano but it was too difficult. Instead, I joined the dance school, the gym club and horseriding classes. I loved them all. I took part in many competitions and have a collection of trophies, medals and rosettes.

From the primary school I moved to the village college. I took some time to get used to being the youngest in a larger school and full of older people. History was my favourite subject. I also liked art but did not like languages as they were too hard to learn. And I was very surprised when I was once given an award for good work in maths !

They did many shows at school but my best was Men in Black. I love dancing and continued with classes after school. We did many shows and they were fun.

I also joined Girl Guides and enjoyed sessions at the swimming club. And to help me with my stresses I started drumming sessions with a member of a rock group called Porcupine Tree. What a therapy it was ! I finished college with a good grade in art. From my college I went to Cambridge Regional College. I joined the special needs unit and worked on many courses. The worst was cooking because I was getting everything wrong.

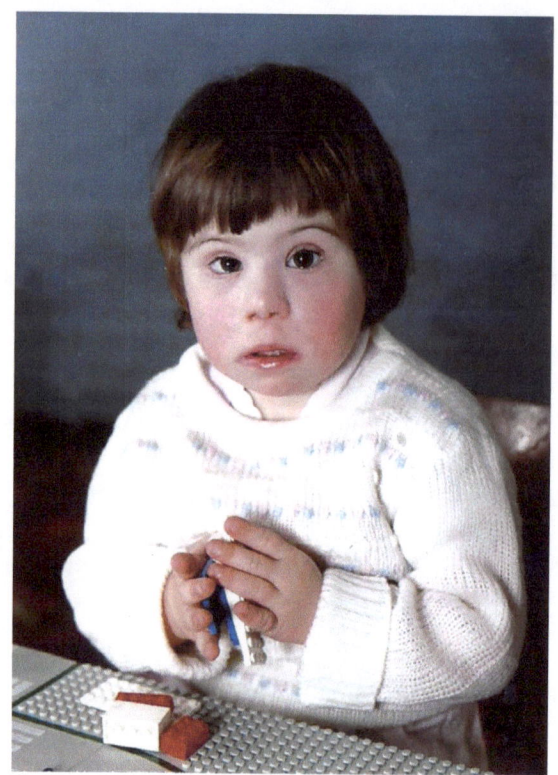

First day at the nursery ...

Party time !

What energy !

A gorgeous flower ...

My old Primary School

This is real fun !

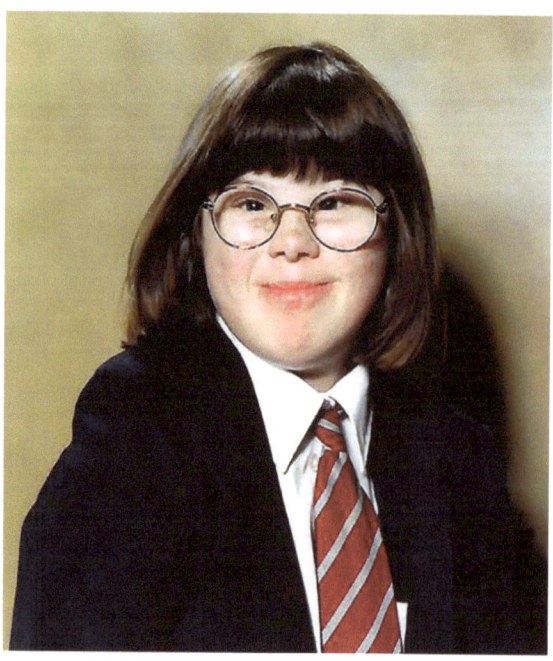

In my college uniform

Chapter 4

MY ART EXHIBITIONS

The most interesting course was creative and expressive arts.

It was run by professional artists who guided us and supported in making all kinds of individual and group art projects.

My tutor and I did a big project together. We sent my paintings to the competition for special needs artists called "In the Frame". One of my pictures was chosen and sent to the exhibition at the Tate Modern Gallery in London and put in their catalogue. It was also shown on the Spider Art website.

I was so proud to see my art on the Tate wall. And later on in many London galleries. The local radio invited me to join the discussion about art. I went but it was too much for me so I only listened to their opinions.

My work was also shown at the College exhibition where the visitors left many positive comments.

Some of my photos were also chosen for a competition in London and I was interviewed by local papers. I felt great as I was showing people my achievements.

Recently, my sculpture won an international top award in England. It is called Emblem- a clay dove – a symbol of peace.

Tate Modern, London

My auto-portraits

Emblem

ArtWorks Together 2023

Emma Anderson, England
Emblem
Best in Show 🌟

Emblem is a ceramic sculpture, created using a combination of press moulding and hand decorating and finishing. The artist, Emma, is a prolific maker in clay, and also loves drama and music. To give a tactile feel, Emma has burnished the work by hand with the back os a spoon. The resulting work is made to be held, fitting perfectly in the palm of your hand to provide a comforting experience.

Lady Dancing in a Sari

Chapter 5

CAMBRIDGE ART STUDIO

I joined the Rowan Foundation art studio 15 years ago. It is a charity for adults with special needs run by professional artists. They have many art groups. For example: woodwork, computer design, textiles, printing, mixed media, ceramics, drama and music.

I tried many but my favourite are ceramics, drama and music.

We do many activities to sponsor the studio: yearly walks along the river Cam, local television interviews and shows in the local theatres. There are many short films on YouTube about us and what we do.

The place is excellent and gives me full freedom in my decisions and choices. I meet my friends and tutors and we talk about everything under the sun. I feel positive and confident. The studio gives me strength, social contact and creative opportunities.

Our pieces of art are shown in public exhibitions at the museums, colleges and fairs. We love to be part of artistic life in Cambridge.

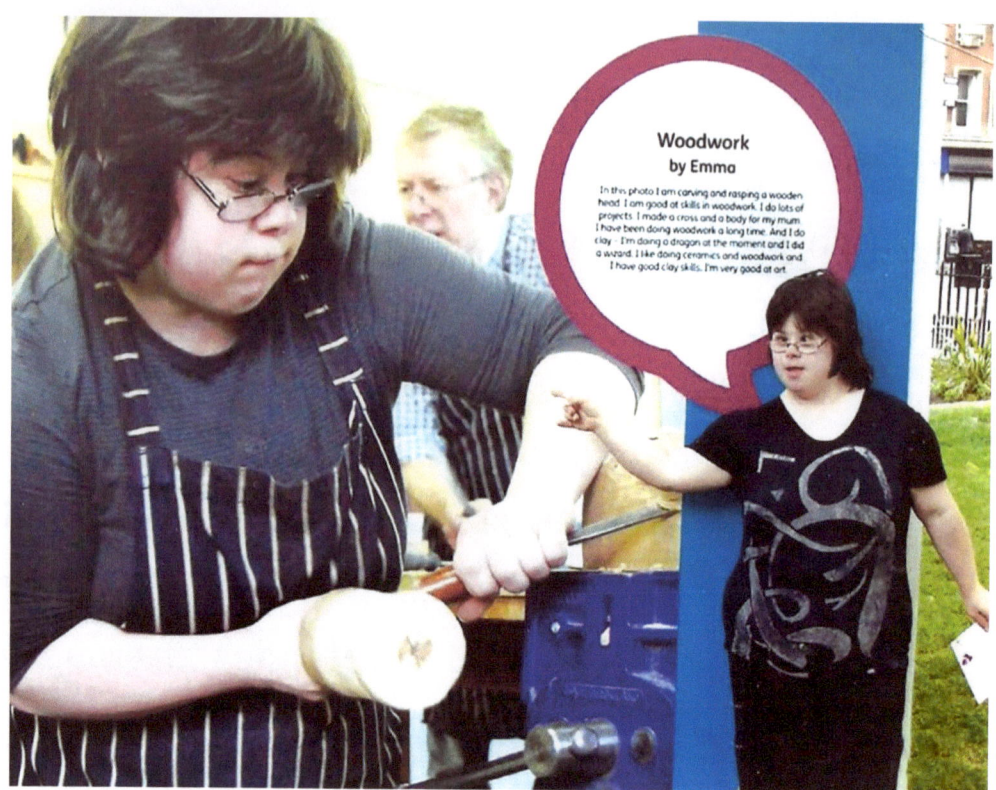

Dedication...

This one is mine...

Russian Babooshka

My mobile tortoise.

Chapter 6

MY HOBBIES

I have always liked watching television. My favourite programmes are: Eastenders, Casualty, Strictly Come Dancing, Pointless and the Hit List. I watched some from the beginning in the 80s as a child because they started at the same time when I was born.

I also am a fan of the 80s music and like rock most. My idol was Steven Tyler from Aerosmith. I saw the group in Hyde Park, London at the concert called "Hard Rock Calling". It was pouring with rain and my mum took a picture of me singing. It won a Snap photo and film competition and was shown in Leicester Square in London. Next time I saw them was at the Download Festival in England.

My favourite football team is Manchester United and I have supported them for years.

I also like horse riding – I have been doing it for a long time. My favourite horse was Polo– because he gave me confidence and always behaved. We won many rosettes in competitions all over England. When I left the team, I was very sorry to leave him because he was such a good company.

I love travelling in England and abroad. We went to many places all over the world by coaches, planes and cruisers. I spend a lot of time looking at our collection of pictures from our trips. It makes me happy to see all the places we visited– lovely memories !

My favourite actor John Altman ...

My version of Steven Tyler ...

Leicester Square, London

Gold again!

Chapter 7

TRAVELLING FUN

I have travelled to many countries.

My best trips in Europe were to Poland, Spain and Madeira. I also love visiting Tunisia, Canda, USA and South America. In the past we flew to Asia and stayed in Thailand, Singapore and Sri Lanka. Australia, New Zealand and Antarctica were on our list, too.

I like spending time in the USA, especially in Florida.

The most attractive was Discovery Cove with dolphins, Universal Studios and NASA centre where they send rockets into space. And the Everglades swamp full of crocodiles. Alaska is also interesting with husky dogsled races and whale watching tours. From there we went on another attraction: the Amtrak train with a glass roof all the way across the States to Chicago.

Some years ago we went on Route 66 by coach. It is the Mother Road following the Gold Rush route. It took us two weeks to cross 9 states. When we got to Amarillo in Texas, I was so happy I started singing "Is this the way to Amarillo?" and everybody joined in! And at the end of the trip, I was given a sheriff's star!

Warsaw Old Town, Poland

Alaskan dogsled race

Give us a kiss...!

We made it !

Chapter 8

I LOVE CRUISING

Because cruises are the easy way to travel. A cruise ship is a hotel on the sea. It stops nearly every day in a different port and makes visiting places very simple: you can get off at every port and visit interesting places in each country.

Once on the cruiser, before you sail away, you have to come to a safety drill in your life jacket.

You can get food in a restaurant or in a self-service buffet. They have shows in the theatre every evening and lots of different quizzes, competitions and a disco– my favourite !

The best cruise I went on recently was the 80s music from Florida to Mexico. There were many bands from those years and every day people dressed up the hippy way and enjoyed oldies like Starship, Berlin and Twisted Sister.

Another cruise, which was fun, sailed from the Hawaii Islands to Sydney, Australia. In the middle of the Pacific we got caught in a typhoon and rocked for a day in every direction. When we crossed the equator we had to follow a custom: to kiss a raw fish to be called "a shellback" – an old and experienced sailor ! And when we arrived in Sydney I was tired and sat on the pavement; an old lady passed by and gave me some dollars – she thought I was begging!

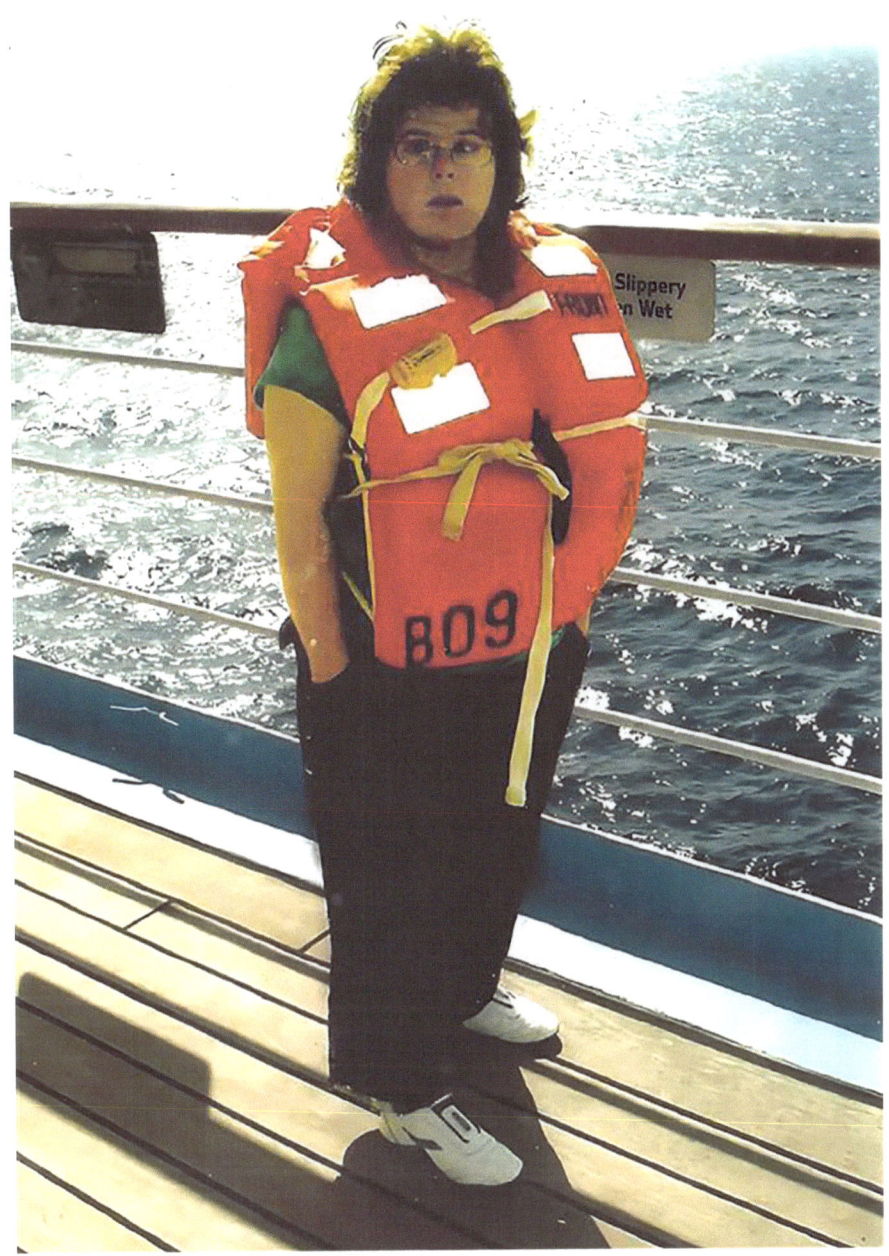

Passed the safety drill ...

Rocking all over the world !

Docked in Victoria, British Columbia

I am a shellback !

Chapter 9

MY FAVOURITE SPORTS

When I was young, I liked going out on my bike, playing on the climbing frames and ice-skating but with age I find these sports more difficult.

I like being on water and especially enjoy speedboating and sailing. And over water loving paragliding and parasailing. I practise indoor sports with my friend every week. We play short tennis, basketball and go swimming. During my travels I went up in a hot air balloon over the desert in Egypt and in a light plane over the fjords in Norway.

On many of my birthdays I play ten pin bowls and always win !

Practising on our local green

Look what I can do !

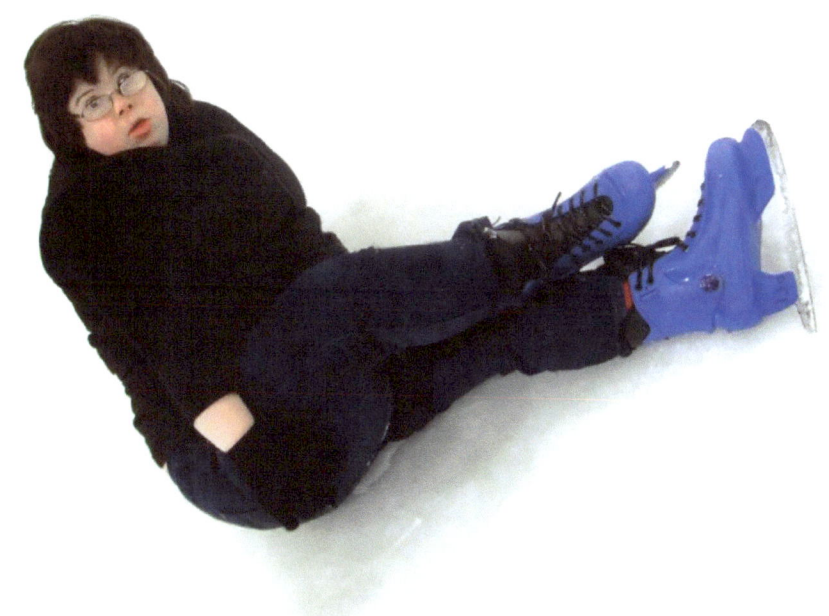

Not again ! It is hard work ...

Paragliding in Tenerife ...

Up, up and away !

Such fun in Tunisia !

Chapter 10

MY LIFE ON FILM

On the day I was born my mum decided to change people's attitude to people with Down syndrome. It was the doctor's negative comment that started her mission.

She fought with the school system to include me in the ordinary school. We won. My art work has been noticed at the highest level and I was included and accepted in the community.

To celebrate our win she made a documentary about my life success called **"the sky is the limit"**. We sent it to many film festivals and have **50 winning awards** from all over the world.

We were invited to the Mexican film festival and went to the screening in front of an audience. They loved it – and I loved the occasion but felt shy in front of the large crowd so mum had to answer the questions.

The trailer is available on YouTube.

Challenge attitude to babies with Down syndrome.

Registration at the festival in Mexico ...

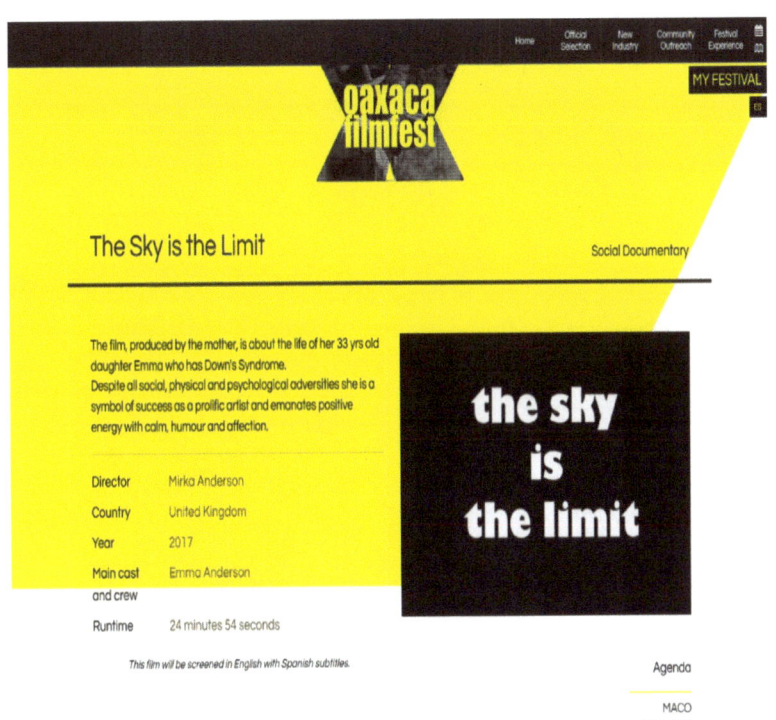

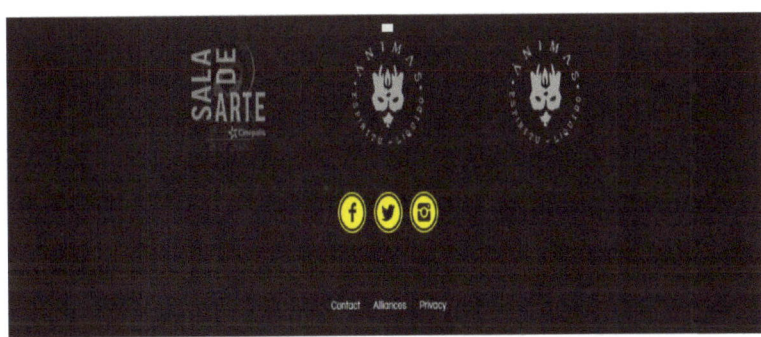

Our first award from Chile ...

World Down Syndrome Day

Every year, on the 21st of March we celebrate the International Down Syndrome Day. The name comes from Dr. Down who first wrote about the condition. People with Down syndrome are born with the condition. They are as different as people without it. But all have similar appearance. Most have communication problems due speech difficulties and slower processing skills. They are perceptive, highly sensitive and just.

The name is the opposite to the abilities of these special and peaceful people. They are definitely not down – they are up and only sky is the limit !

By mirkieran@hotmail.com
www.emmaanderson.org